The Courage to Face my Inner Self

The Courage to Face my Inner Self

I would like to thank my sister, Laurie, for always being there for me, no matter what. Ron, for making my life entirely enjoyable and teaching me the true value of love. My children, for the support and understanding they have shown through the years and for validating the good I have done in my life.

The Courage to Face my Inner Self

The Courage to Face my Inner Self

The Courage to Face my Inner Self

Written by:

Angela Levitan

The Courage to Face my Inner Self

The Courage to Face my Inner Self

THE STRENGTH TO SURVIVE,

THE WILLPOWER TO SUCCEED,

AND THE COURAGE TO

KNOW THE DIFFERENCE.

The Courage to Face my Inner Self

The Courage to Face my Inner Self

Prologue

Odd, strange, weird, overactive, fun, crazy, mad, mean, cranky, foul, difficult, grandiose, scary, troublesome, energetic, strong, bull headed, smart, and the list could go

The Courage to Face my Inner Self

ON AND ON. THESE ARE ALL WORDS THAT DESCRIBE THE MANIC STAGE IN BI-POLAR DISORDER. THIS STAGE CAN DIFFER FROM TIME TO TIME OR FROM PERSON TO PERSON, RANGING FROM A HAPPY ON TOP OF THE WORLD PORTRAYAL TO A MEAN CRABBY PORTRAYAL. THE TIME ASSOCIATED WITH THE MANIC PHASE CAN LAST MINUTES IN RAPID CYCLING TO DAYS OR MONTHS IN A NORMAL CYCLE (IF YOU CAN CALL ANYTHING ABOUT THIS DISORDER, NORMAL). THIS PARTICULAR PART OF THE BI-POLAR CYCLE CAN FEEL GREAT AT TIMES, LEADING US TO FEEL PRODUCTIVE WITH THE ABILITY TO

The Courage to Face my Inner Self

ACCOMPLISH ANYTHING. IT MAY ALSO LEAD US INTO TROUBLE SUCH AS LEGAL PROBLEMS OR UNFAVORABLE IMPRESSIONS WITH OTHERS. THEN WE CRASH!

LAZY, SAD, UNINTERESTED, LACK OF AMBITION, TEARFUL, SUICIDAL, NO MOTIVATION, SELF-DESTRUCTIVE, AND TIRED, ARE ALL WORDS USED TO DESCRIBE THE DEPRESSIVE SIDE OF BI-POLAR DISORDER. FEELINGS OF WORTHLESSNESS HAPPEN FREQUENTLY DURING THIS PHASE AND CAN LEAD TO MAJOR PROBLEMS SUCH AS ATTEMPTED SUICIDE OR LASTING SELF-WORTH ISSUES. CONFUSION IS ANOTHER FACTOR WITH THIS STAGE, I WAS ON TOP

The Courage to Face my Inner Self

OF THE WORLD AND NOW I AM WORTHLESS, THIS TENDS TO PLAY HARD ON OUR MINDS. UNFORTUNATELY, THIS PHASE ALSO HAS THE EFFECT OF LEAVING THE GREATEST IMPRESSION ON ME AS A WHOLE. I LEAVE THIS PHASE BELIEVING WHOLE-HEARTEDLY THAT THIS IS WHO I AM. DO I THINK CLEARER DURING DEPRESSION? I AM NOT SURE, I JUST KNOW THAT I FEEL WORSE ABOUT MYSELF WHEN I LEAVE THIS STAGE.

ANYONE THAT HAS BEEN THROUGH ANY MENTAL DISORDER KNOWS OR AT LEAST HAS A GOOD IDEA HOW OTHERS VIEW US. WE ARE THE PEOPLE THAT ARE LOOKING FOR ATTENTION, FAKING IT. WE

The Courage to Face my Inner Self

ARE LAZY OR MAYBE WE ARE SO CRAZY IN THEIR EYES THAT THEY AVOID US ALTOGETHER. THE FEAR IN SOME PEOPLE'S EYES IS PALPABLE, YOU CAN FEEL IT AND IT IS SAD. THERE IS ALSO DENIAL, THE NOTHING IS WRONG WITH YOU PEOPLE, IT IS ALL IN YOUR HEAD. I CAN TELL EVERYONE I KNOW THAT THIS DISORDER IS VERY REAL; IT IS NOT JUST IN MY HEAD. TRUST ME IF I WAS JUST IMAGINING THIS DISORDER, IT WOULD BE GONE BY NOW. AFTER ALL THE TIMES I HAVE TRIED TO PUSH IT OUT OF MY MIND, PRETEND IT WASN'T AN ISSUE, AND TRIED EVERY CURE THE DOCTORS GAVE ME,

The Courage to Face my Inner Self

IF IT WAS JUST IN MY HEAD, IT WOULD HAVE BEEN GONE WAY BEFORE NOW.

I WAS DIAGNOSED IN 2005 WITH BI-POLAR TYPE 1, RAPID CYCLING AFTER MANY YEARS OF STRUGGLING AND MANY MORE YEARS OF DAMAGE. LOOKING BACK, MY FIRST DEFINITIVE SIGNS WERE IN MY TEENAGE YEARS, BUT I AM SURE THERE WERE SIGNS OR SYMPTOMS IN MY EARLIER YEARS. THE EXPERTS ARE THE ONES THAT I ALLUDE TO FOR ANSWERS, BUT THEN AGAIN SCIENCE IS NOT PERFECT AND I KNOW MYSELF AND WHAT I SEE FIRST-HAND IS WHAT I TEND TO BELIEVE.

The Courage to Face my Inner Self

I AM WRITING THIS BOOK TO HELP OTHERS ALONG THEIR JOURNEY. I CAN HONESTLY SAY THAT I HAVE OBTAINED A POINT IN MY LIFE WHERE MY BI-POLAR IS NOT SUCH A DRAMATIC ISSUE ANYMORE. IS IT BECAUSE I AM NOW IN MY 40'S OR MAYBE I HAVE JUST LEARNED MY OWN WAY OF DEALING. I CAN'T HELP WONDERING IF IT IS JUST THAT I MAY BE SO FAR GONE AS TO NOT RECOGNIZE THAT I AM JUST UTTERLY INSANE AND NOT SEEING WHAT IS OBVIOUS TO OTHERS. THAT WOULD BE A BAD THING. IN WRITING THIS, I BY NO MEANS CLAIM TO KNOW EVERYTHING OR THAT I KNOW WHAT THE DOCTORS DO, JUST THAT I AM GIVING A

The Courage to Face my Inner Self

FIRST-HAND EXPERIENCE OF WHAT I HAVE WENT THROUGH AND THE THINGS I NOTICED ALONG THE WAY.

The Courage to Face my Inner Self

The Courage to Face my Inner Self

Myself;

The only person who truly understands me

The Courage to Face my Inner Self

Chapter 1

Who I am

If you ask anyone that knows me, the answer tends to be fun, nice, but unpredictable. That's me in a nutshell. Over the years I have

The Courage to Face my Inner Self

morphed into more of the nice category and it works for me. You will have to excuse my writing technique due to the unpredictable part of my nature; I find that I tend to write with my moods, crying at times and energetic in others. It is the nature of the beast and I have also found that if I roll with my moods, I get more done. So when I tend to go off subject, don't worry, I will pick it back up some time soon. Those who have gained an understanding of the disease understand whole-heartedly. Those that haven't will hopefully

The Courage to Face my Inner Self

gain an understanding and the possibility of being able to relate. It is my hopes that this book will give other bi-polars hope and possibly some ideas that will make life a little better in the long run.

Getting back to the subject, who am I? Well, I am female, 42, with three grown children. I am bright and meticulous, honest and kind, crazy and sober. I have been diagnosed with bi-polar type 1, rapid cycling, anxiety disorder, and OCD. The OCD part comes into play because I worry about everything, including the stuff

The Courage to Face my Inner Self

I have no control over. I also come back into my home to check and make sure I have turned things off, the clothes dryer in particular, but I usually go through the whole routine of checking the stove and the doors too. My nasty bad habit is smoking like a chimney. I find that if I do not have my cigarettes, I take heads off. It is not a pleasant habit and I try on a regular basis to quit, which so far has not worked. Currently, I live with the most compassionate man I have ever met, even though he is blissfully unaware

The Courage to Face my Inner Self

OF WHAT BI-POLAR MEANS, IN FACT HE DOESN'T THINK THAT MENTAL ILLNESS EVEN EXISTS, WHICH HELPS ME KEEP MYSELF IN CHECK MOST DAYS BUT WE WILL GET INTO THAT LATER.

I RECEIVED MY DIAGNOSIS IN 1996 DURING A PARTICULARLY BAD BOUT OF INSOMNIA. TWO WEEKS WITHOUT SLEEPING BUT A FEW MINUTES HERE AND THERE IS ENOUGH TO PUT ANYONE IN THE HOSPITAL. UP UNTIL THIS TIME, I KNEW I WAS DIFFERENT, BUT DID NOT HAVE THE SLIGHTEST CLUE THAT IT WAS AS SERIOUS AS THE DOCTORS TOLD ME. I MAY HAVE BEEN ABLE TO GUESS IF I WOULD HAVE

The Courage to Face my Inner Self

known that mental illness ran in my family. My fraternal grandmother was schizophrenic, my father was bi-polar and my sister has major depression. I guess this means I get it honestly.

Much of this may have defined who I am, but other factors played a big role. It is uncanny how a person can look back on their time on earth and see so much, but during the making of our lives, we see nothing but the here and now. If only I could go back, knowing what I now know,

The Courage to Face my Inner Self

THINGS COULD HAVE BEEN SO MUCH BETTER. I KNOW, HINDSIGHT, RIGHT.

The Courage to Face my Inner Self

The Courage to Face my Inner Self

I shake, I shiver,

My body throbs,

It's as normal as me.

The Courage to Face my Inner Self

Chapter 2

Feeling the symptoms

If someone was to ask my experienced advice in this horrific disorder, I would say it is a dysfunctional reaction to extreme

The Courage to Face my Inner Self

STRESS. I SAY THIS BECAUSE I NOW LIVE FAIRLY FREE OF STRESS AND MY SYMPTOMS. THE MOST DIFFICULT TIMES I HAD DURING MY YEARS WAS WHEN I HAD THREE CHILDREN TO RAISE, BILLS PILING UP, LAZY GOOD FOR NOTHING PARTNERS, AND LITERALLY NO SUPPORT FROM MY FAMILY. THE WORLD WAS RIGID AND SCARY. I WORRIED ABOUT EVERYTHING FROM SCRAPED KNEES TO KEEPING MY JOB. THE HORRIBLE SINKING FEELING THAT I COULD NOT ESCAPE WAS DRIVING MY FEELINGS, EMOTIONS AND HEALTH. I CRINGE AS I REMEMBER THAT FEELING AND STRUGGLE WITH FINDING A DESCRIPTIVE

The Courage to Face my Inner Self

EXAMPLE OF HOW TERRIBLE THE FEELING WAS.

THE FEELING THAT I REMEMBER MOST WOULD BEGIN WITH AN EXTREME HUNGRY TYPE OF FEELING, SOME EXPLAIN IT AS BUTTERFLIES, OTHERS A TWISTING FEELING IN THEIR STOMACH. I WOULD FEEL LIKE THIS BUT WOULD LOSE MY APPETITE; MOST TIMES I WOULD HAVE FEELINGS THAT ACCOMPANIED THE FEELING IN MY STOMACH, SUCH AS A HEADACHE, SHAKING, OR A FEELING LIKE MY EYES WERE GOING TO ROLL BACK IN MY HEAD. SOMETIMES I COULD FEEL MY HEARTBEAT AND AT OTHER TIMES I WOULD SHAKE. LATER IN MY LIFE, I

The Courage to Face my Inner Self

started to develop diarrhea every time I entered this phase. When I would feel these symptoms was usually when I was entering my depressive state of the disorder. It was an anxious reaction to the knowledge that I was falling into depression.

My depression was very hard to handle. I would start my day by forcing myself out of bed in the morning and doing the bare minimum to prepare for work. I would put on sweats, throw my hair back in a ponytail and go, no shower, no

The Courage to Face my Inner Self

MAKEUP, NO HAIRSTYLING, JUST WHAT I HAD TO DO TO GET THROUGH THE DAY. I WOULD GET SO TIRED DURING THE DAY THAT I WOULD FEEL MYSELF FALLING ASLEEP AT MY DESK AND ALWAYS FELT LIKE I WAS DOING SOMETHING WRONG, EVEN THOUGH I WAS VERY GOOD AT MY JOB. DURING THESE TIMES, MY KIDS WOULD RECOGNIZE MY DEPRESSION BEFORE I DID AND AS THEY AGED, THEY WOULD START TO TELL ME WHEN THEY NOTICED MAJOR CHANGES IN MY BEHAVIOR. IT WAS SHOCKING AT FIRST THAT I COULD NOT EVEN RECOGNIZE MAJOR CHANGES IN MYSELF. I WOULD ALSO HIDE, NOT

The Courage to Face my Inner Self

ANSWERING THE DOOR OR TELEPHONE, IGNORING FAMILY AND FRIENDS DURING THIS TIME. EVEN THOUGH I FELT SO BAD, I WOULD NOT ATTEMPT GOING TO THE DOCTOR DURING THESE PERIODS, I SAVED THAT UNTIL I WAS IN A MANIC PHASE.

MY MANIC PHASES WERE THE BEST WITH THE EXCEPTION OF NOT BEING ABLE TO SLEEP MUCH. I WAS ON TOP OF THE WORLD, COULD DO ANYTHING, I ALWAYS SEEMED TO CONVINCE MYSELF THAT I WAS OF SOUND BODY AND MIND, NOTHING WOULD GET ME DOWN. I EXCELLED AT ANYTHING I PUT MY MIND TO AND HAD SO MUCH ENERGY THAT IT WAS RIDICULOUS.

The Courage to Face my Inner Self

My biggest drawback during this time was the ever alluding sleep I needed to stay in this stage. Sometimes I would sleep 4 or 5 hours a day, other times I would sleep 4 or 5 hours a week. This lack of sleep would eventually catch up to me and I would crash back down to the depression phase and everything would start all over again.

I think the worst part of my disorder was the way others treated me. I would tell someone I was not feeling well and they would appear sympathetic, but the comments of

The Courage to Face my Inner Self

"JUST SNAP OUT OF IT" OR "EVERYONE FEELS THAT WAY FROM TIME TO TIME" OR A WEALTH OF OTHER REPLIES COULD HURT AND MAKE ME FEEL AS IF I SHOULD BE ASHAMED, AND I WAS FOR MANY YEARS ASHAMED OF ME. I DON'T KNOW HOW MANY TIMES I WOULD PUT A PAMPHLET OR BOOK IN FRONT OF THOSE I LOVED AND ASK THEM TO READ IT WITH THE HOPES OF FINALLY BEING UNDERSTOOD, BUT IT BECAME OBVIOUS OVER THE YEARS THAT NOT ONE OF THEM READ THE INFORMATION. I NEVER LOOKED FOR ANYTHING OUT OF ANY OF THEM BESIDES UNDERSTANDING, BUT THAT WAS TOO MUCH TO ASK. LOOKING BACK, I

The Courage to Face my Inner Self

AM UNSURE IF THEIR UNDERSTANDING COULD HAVE HELPED ME, BUT I DO KNOW IT WOULD HAVE HELPED ME DEAL AND THE WAY I FELT ABOUT MYSELF. THE ONLY EXCEPTION WAS MY SISTER, WHOM SUFFERS FROM HER OWN MENTAL HEALTH ISSUES, SHE WAS MY ONLY SANITY IN MY INSANELY LEANING LIFE. THANK YOU, SIS.

Written by Angela Levitan

The Courage to Face my Inner Self

The Courage to Face my Inner Self

Looking back can

Ease our minds

Or

Torment our souls.

The Courage to Face my Inner Self

Chapter 3

The Early Years

Looking back, there is not much that I remember as a small child. My first real memories were in about sixth grade. I do know that I was a

The Courage to Face my Inner Self

DIFFICULT CHILD, I HAD NIGHT TERRORS, I WAS A SLEEPWALKER, AND TEMPER TANTRUMS WERE FREQUENT IN OUR HOUSE. I WAS SICK QUITE A BIT AND HAD SOME MAJOR ISSUES WITH KIDNEY INFECTIONS. I HAD A DIFFICULT TIME MAKING AND KEEPING FRIENDS. SOME TEACHERS HAD DIFFICULTIES WITH MY ATTITUDE AND INSISTENCE THAT I KNEW IT ALL. I WAS THE OLDEST OF THREE CHILDREN AND AS BOSSY AS COULD BE. IT WAS NOT ALL BAD THOUGH, I WAS A FAST LEARNER AND USUALLY EXCELLED AT ANYTHING I PUT MY MIND TO. I FINISHED WHATEVER I SET OUT TO DO, AND HAD AN ARTISTIC SIDE TO ME

THAT PROVIDED MANY HOURS OF ENTERTAINMENT.

Where my memories began, my parents' marriage ended. It turned out dad was an alcoholic and mom was seeing another man, which really set him off on a rampage. He went through our home, when mom had taken us kids and left, with a baseball bat, an axe, and a butcher knife. The neighbors said it sounded like a bunch of wild Indians were in our home, but the police would do nothing about it due to it being his own property. He destroyed everything, and when I say

The Courage to Face my Inner Self

EVERYTHING THAT IS WHAT I MEAN, KITCHEN COUNTERS, FLOORS, WINDOWS, FURNITURE, BEDS, TV'S, EVEN CUTTING OUR DOGS FOOT IN THE PROCESS. I HAVE ONLY SEEN MY FATHER ONCE SINCE THE DIVORCE AND THAT WAS A VISIT TO HIM IN JAIL. CURRENTLY, I HAVE BEEN UNABLE TO LOCATE HIM. I WOULD LIKE TO KNOW THAT HE GETS A DECENT BURIAL AND SUCH AND MAYBE DELVE INTO HIS MIND IN ORDER TO UNDERSTAND WHAT FAMILY HISTORY WE SHARE.

NEEDLESS TO SAY, THEIR DIVORCE STARTED A WHOLE NEW CHAPTER IN MY LIFE. WITH MOM BEING SINGLE, SHE WAS

The Courage to Face my Inner Self

BARELY ABLE TO KEEP A ROOF OVER OUR HEADS. I WAS THE OLDEST OF THREE CHILDREN AND THE CHILDCARE FELL HEAVILY ON MY SHOULDERS. I LEARNED TO COOK, CLEAN, WIPE FACES AND HANDS, GIVE BATHS, ENSURE THE DOORS WERE LOCKED, READ BEDTIME STORIES AND ANY OTHER THING A PARENT DOES. AT THIS TIME, MOM STARTED GETTING MEAN, MAYBE IT WAS THE STRESS OR MAYBE SHE HAD MENTAL PROBLEMS AS WELL, I STILL TO THIS DAY AM UNSURE OF THE REASONING. WHAT I DO KNOW IS THAT ALL THREE OF US WOULD DO THE NORMAL THINGS KIDS DO TO GET INTO TROUBLE WITH OUR PARENTS,

The Courage to Face my Inner Self

but Mom would go ballistic and lash out hard. It was at this time that I decided that protecting my sister and brother was more important than protecting my own self. When I had my own kids, I would tell them that Grandma was sick and to ignore some of the comments she would make to them, mean hurtful things that I was afraid would damage their self-confidence later in life.

After many bruises, berating, and name calling, at the age of 14, I found a way out. I began my first job at a little ice cream place. The money I

The Courage to Face my Inner Self

EARNED WENT DIRECTLY TO HELP THE HOUSEHOLD, CREATING A MUCH EASIER PARENT TO GET ALONG WITH. AT 16 I DROPPED OUT OF SCHOOL AND HELPED OUT WITH TWO FULL TIME JOBS, IMPROVING OUR LOT IN LIFE EVEN MORE. IT WAS DURING THIS TIME THAT MY FIRST SYMPTOMS STARTED TO APPEAR, EVEN THOUGH I HAD NO WAY OF KNOWING THEY WERE SYMPTOMS OF A SERIOUS PROBLEM. I JUST ATTRIBUTED THEM TO THE FEELING THAT I WAS ALWAYS IN TROUBLE, EVEN THOUGH I WAS A RELATIVELY GOOD KID. MY STOMACH WOULD KNOT UP OR I WOULD GET THAT BUTTERFLY FEELING IN MY

The Courage to Face my Inner Self

stomach every time I headed home. At times my heart would race and I started worrying that I was going to die soon, that I had a serious problem. Mentioning this to Mom brought no relief, she just said I was blowing my symptoms out of proportion and would ignore my insistence that it was more. I even learned how to cook at this time because I was afraid that she hated me so much that she would poison us. So this is how I lived out the rest of my childhood.

Even though I dropped out of school to help out and get my Mom

The Courage to Face my Inner Self

off my back, it was not the only contributing factor. Studies were so boring that I would practically fall asleep sitting up, not saying that I received good grades because I didn't, I was just too bored to pay attention at all. Making and keeping friends was also difficult. When I made a friend I would tend to become clingy and so wrapped up in the friend that there was no room for others. This, in turn, tended to turn off my new friends at some point, leaving me searching for that next best friend. Most of my peers called me strange

The Courage to Face my Inner Self

AND HAD NOTHING TO DO WITH ME. I NEVER UNDERSTOOD WHY AND STILL DON'T TO THIS DAY.

LOOKING BACK I DO SEE THAT MY REACTIONS WERE WAY OFF COURSE IN MANY INSTANCES AND MY MOODS WERE PROBABLY VERY EVIDENT TO ANYONE CONSIDERED "NORMAL". TO THIS DAY, I HONESTLY CAN SAY I HAVE ONE FRIEND FROM MY CHILDHOOD. WE MET IN 4TH GRADE AND I THINK I JUST GREW ON HER, NOT TO MENTION THAT SHE MOVED AWAY IN 6TH GRADE AND THE DISTANCE MAY HAVE KEPT HER FROM NOTICING MY DEFECTS.

The Courage to Face my Inner Self

The Courage to Face my Inner Self

NEW BEGINNINGS SOMETIMES

LEAD TO BITTER ENDS.

The Courage to Face my Inner Self

Chapter 4

Starting my own family

I met my first husband at 17 and moved in with him a few weeks before I turned 18. We started a family immediately and ended up with three

The Courage to Face my Inner Self

CHILDREN BY THE TIME I WAS 21. I KNOW CRAZY, RIGHT? I WOULD NEVER CHANGE IT, MY KIDS ARE GREAT AND I WAS YOUNG ENOUGH TO ENJOY THEM. WE SORT OF GREW UP TOGETHER. WHEN I HAD MY SECOND CHILD, I STARTED TO HAVE PANIC ATTACKS. THEY PROGRESSED SO RAPIDLY AND LEFT ME UNABLE TO DRIVE FOR ABOUT SIX MONTHS. WHERE WE LIVED, I HAD TO DRIVE ACROSS A SMALL BRIDGE OVER THE FREEWAY TO GET ANYWHERE AND I HAD STARTED TO PICTURE DRIVING OFF OF IT EVERY TIME I DROVE OVER IT. THIS SCARED ME AND LEFT ME IN AN ANXIETY ATTACKS WHENEVER I THOUGHT ABOUT IT. I ENDED

The Courage to Face my Inner Self

UP BEING SENT TO A PSYCHIATRIST FOR THE FIRST TIME IN MY LIFE. I WENT TO A FEW SESSIONS WHERE I ENDED UP COUNSELING MY COUNSELOR, BECAME BORED AND QUIT GOING. I WAS ALWAYS GOOD AT LISTENING AND TURNING THINGS AROUND TO WHERE OTHER PEOPLE TALKED. THE PRESCRIPTION THE DOCTOR GAVE ME NEVER SEEMED TO DO ANY GOOD, SO I DIDN'T TAKE THEM AND JUST DEALT WITH THE ATTACKS UNTIL WE MOVED A FEW MONTHS LATER. YOU COULDN'T HAVE CONVINCED ME AT THIS TIME THAT THERE WAS ANYTHING MENTALLY WRONG WITH ME; IT WAS THE WORLD, STRESS, OTHER PEOPLE ACTIONS. THE

The Courage to Face my Inner Self

WHOLE WORLD WAS WRONG AND I WAS RIGHT.

As my marriage progressed, major events eventually led to our breakup. My husband started getting abusive, not towards me, but towards the kids. Fracturing my daughter cheekbone was the final straw. He never tried to hurt me, not once during our whole marriage. I think he was afraid to get physical with me because I had such a bad temper, he was afraid of me. Around the same time my daughter started having seizures on a regular basis. They called it a seizure disorder and gave no real explanation as to why they were happening. I attribute some of her problems to her father's actions. She is also blind in one eye due to the injury she sustained by his hand.

The divorce happened at a time in my life where in all honesty I should have broken because the stress level was unbelievable. I had not worked since having my kids and the prospects were not good. Having no education and no real experience, I was doomed to fail. This is about the time that I can look back and see the

The Courage to Face my Inner Self

RAPID CYCLING ASPECT OF MY DISORDER. I WOULD GET DRESSED IN THE MORNING, ALL HYPED UP TO FIND A JOB, DRIVE TO PUT IN AN APPLICATION AND END UP SITTING IN MY CAR FOR HOURS. I WOULD BREAK DOWN CRYING, THEN WAIT UNTIL I LOOKED AND FELT NORMAL AGAIN, THEN GO IN AND GIVE THEM EVERYTHING I HAD. THIS PROCESS WOULD REPEAT ITSELF MANY TIMES BEFORE I FINALLY LANDED A JOB. I WAS DRAINED, TIRED, SCARED, BUT ON TOP OF THE WORLD.

THE JOB I FIRST LANDED WAS IN SALES AND REQUIRED 12 HOUR DAYS, LEAVING ME JUGGLING TWO SHIFTS OF BABYSITTERS. I

The Courage to Face my Inner Self

worked 6 days a week trying to pay the bills and keep my family together. My ex-husband refused to pay child support and it would be many years until the state caught up with him. Eventually I lost the house. My kids ended up staying with my sister and her family for a while and I ended up at my Mothers. No one in my family would let us stay together; it was either the kids or me. To this day, I really have no idea why. Being split with my kids brought me into a major depression and I ended up losing my sales job due to no shows and poor

The Courage to Face my Inner Self

sales. Back to square one, I ended up finding two waitressing jobs and worked my tail off trying to earn enough to get my kids back.

The Courage to Face my Inner Self

The Courage to Face my Inner Self

The Courage to Face my Inner Self

Sometimes we must wipe

The slate clean,

Other times we must

Tell ourselves to

Never forget.

The Courage to Face my Inner Self

Chapter 5

Starting over

It is at this time that I met my second husband, the one who broke open the can of worms and led me to my diagnosis. At first everything was wonderful and I jumped at his

The Courage to Face my Inner Self

suggestion that my kids and I come live with him. He had a self-supporting job and with my job, we could make a fairly nice life. We ended up getting married quickly and settled in. Two weeks later, he quit his job, claiming a work injury which eventually led to disability and social security. He also started getting abusive, verbally and physically. When verbal abuse starts, it is usually started so gradually and with such precision that it is easy to not realize what is happening to you. I think this is especially true if you are battling an

The Courage to Face my Inner Self

UNDIAGNOSED OR TREATED MENTAL DISORDER. IT WAS EASY FOR HIM TO START PUTTING BLAME ON ME FOR EVERY LITTLE THING, INCLUDING HIS OWN FAILINGS. IT WAS MY FAULT, I WAS THE BAD ONE, AND I MADE HIM DO IT. WHEN HE FINALLY HAD ME BELIEVING THAT EVERYTHING WAS MY FAULT, HE STARTED ON THE KIDS. I WAS SO WRAPPED UP IN MY OWN PRIVATE HELL THAT I DID NOT EVEN REALIZE THAT THE KIDS WERE SUFFERING JUST AS MUCH.

A YEAR AFTER MARRYING, I LANDED A REALLY GOOD JOB. IT PAID TRIPLE WHAT I HAD EVER MADE AND WAS THE TYPE OF JOB MANY PEOPLE ARE ENVIOUS OF. I

The Courage to Face my Inner Self

remember thinking to myself that this was it, I couldn't be blamed for our problems any more, and money would solve them. I had finally succeeded and so would my marriage. I was so wrong. When things did not change, the frustration level ended up being so bad that I found myself lashing out at everyone and everything. I broke dishes, windows, kicked in doors, told strangers off at the store, followed drivers home that had cut me off. I thank God for watching over me, because I never got into legal problems, but I came close.

The Courage to Face my Inner Self

I WILL NEVER FORGET THE FIRST OF MANY DAYS THAT LED TO MY ADMITTANCE TO THE HOSPITAL AND MY DIAGNOSIS. I HAD A DIFFICULT DAY AND WAS TIRED. I WENT TO BED AND MY MIND WOULD NOT SHUT OFF. I LAID IN BED ALL NIGHT, TRYING TO FIGURE OUT WHY I DID NOT FEEL TIRED. I GOT UP IN THE MORNING AND FELT FINE, WENT TO WORK AND CAME HOME EXHAUSTED PHYSICALLY. THIS REPEATED ITSELF FOR TWO WEEKS STRAIGHT. I FELT GREAT IN MY MIND, BUT MY BODY WANTED TO DROP AND I KNEW THEN THAT I WAS IN TROUBLE. I WAS PALE, HAD BAGS UNDER MY EYES THE SIZE OF GOLF BALLS, AND

The Courage to Face my Inner Self

was starting to get muddled up in my mind. I ended up driving myself to the hospital. My ex would not take me. The doctors took one look at me, asked a couple questions and admitted me to the psych ward for an evaluation. They gave me something that knocked me out and I finally slept. I ended up in an outpatient hospital or day hospital where I finally got my diagnosis.

Over the period of six months I ended up in an outpatient program three times due to medicine changes and so forth. I remember many times,

The Courage to Face my Inner Self

LOOKING AROUND ME AT THE OTHER PATIENTS AND THINKING I DID NOT BELONG, THEY WERE CRAZY, STRANGE, AND JUST NOT LIKE ME. I WAS WRONG, AFTER MY MEDICATION WAS STABILIZED AND PSYCHOTHERAPY TAUGHT ME A THING OR TWO, I REALIZED THAT I WAS JUST LIKE THESE PEOPLE. THIS WAS HOW THE WORLD SAW ME AND IT WAS ALSO THE REASON I BELIEVED EVERYTHING MY HUSBAND SAID. THAT WAS THE TIME I REALIZED THAT I WAS IN MUCH MORE TROUBLE THAN JUST MY HEALTH.

MY CLARITY OF MIND TOOK A LONG TIME TO LEAD TO MY LEAVING AND

The Courage to Face my Inner Self

DIVORCING MY HUSBAND. I LEFT THE HOSPITAL PROGRAM WITH TWO ANTIPSYCHOTICS, A MOOD STABILIZER, AND AN ANTI-DEPRESSANT. I WAS DRUGGED UP TO THE HILT. I PERFORMED MY JOB AND DAILY FUNCTIONS, BUT AT A BARE MINIMUM. I ONLY FOCUSED ON ONE THING AT A TIME, EVERYTHING ELSE CEASED TO EXIST. THE FEW TIMES THAT THE FOG DID LIFT, I WOULD THINK IT WAS ALL THE DRUGS, GO OFF MY MEDICATION AND END UP BACK AT SQUARE ONE. THIS CYCLE SEEMED TO GO ON FOREVER. MY HUSBAND'S ABUSE FINALLY CROSSED THE LINE TO PHYSICAL AND I DECIDED I HAD TO LEAVE IF I WANTED

The Courage to Face my Inner Self

TO LIVE. IT TOOK ME AWHILE AND TOOK THE HELP OF A FRIEND TO GET OUT ONCE AND FOR ALL.

The Courage to Face my Inner Self

Never, ever give

A good friend

A reason to leave.

The Courage to Face my Inner Self

Chapter 6

Marriage number 3

Many medication adjustments and psycho-therapy sessions finally led to the ability to function well on my own. My thought process returned and I attributed the mental fog I had to the stress of my last marriage.

The Courage to Face my Inner Self

Shortly after my job came to an end, my position was being moved overseas and I was offered a buy-out and it was highly advised that I take it. I did and bought a little place of my own, paid cash so I would not have to worry about too much as far as financials go. I was happy, my children were finally happy and I kept them in the same school, so it was a win-win situation. I had yet to realize the ramifications my last marriage had on my children and that light bulb didn't go off for some time to come. I was

STILL HEALING AND THAT WAS ALL I COULD DO.

My third marriage came as a surprise of sorts. We decided to live together to see how things went and lived together for about two years. We eventually got married and looked forward to a lifetime relationship. He was a good husband and the kids loved him. He worked hard and together we provided more than I was ever able to provide them on my own. I started to worry less about paying bills and putting food

The Courage to Face my Inner Self

ON THE TABLE AND MORE ABOUT LIFE IN GENERAL.

With a calmer, less stressed life I decided that it was time I saw what reducing my medications would do and slowly started to wean myself off of them. I did great until I came to the one that put me to sleep at night. I will not mention the name of these medications because in all fairness, they may work different on others than they did on me and should be doctor directed. It was an antipsychotic and I tried initially to take them every other day, which did

The Courage to Face my Inner Self

NOT WORK. I THEN TRIED CUTTING THEM IN HALF AND THAT DIDN'T WORK EITHER. IN FACT, BOTH TRIALS ONLY MADE ME SEEM WORSE. I COULD NOT SLEEP AT ALL. I EVENTUALLY STARTED CUTTING SMALL SLIVERS OFF OF THIS PILL AND OVER THE PERIOD OF SIX MONTHS WEANED MYSELF OFF. I COULD FINALLY SLEEP WITHOUT ANY MEDICATION. THE FEELING OF FINALLY BEING FREE OF MEDICATIONS WAS SCARY AND EXHILARATING AT THE SAME TIME, I HAD FINALLY DONE IT. THIS IS NOT RECOMMENDED BY THE WAY, JUST MY STORY AND MY OWN DECISIONS, WHETHER RIGHT OF WRONG.

The Courage to Face my Inner Self

My third marriage lasted a few years, when we finally mutually decided that we had nothing in common anymore. We split up amicably and remain friends to this day. I still think he is a wonderful person and we both cherish the friendship we have retained.

The Courage to Face my Inner Self

The Courage to Face my Inner Self

The Courage to Face my Inner Self

Rocks can be crushed,

Broken, or chipped.

Therefore when you

Find a nice shiny one,

Keep it safe always.

The Courage to Face my Inner Self

Chapter 7

My rock

My rock, that's what I call my partner now. We cohabitate due to our past hurts and mistakes. Gun-shy and as skittish as two doe's, we tend to prefer the freedom to walk away if things go south. I honestly think he is

The Courage to Face my Inner Self

THE ONE I SHOULD HAVE FOUND MANY YEARS PREVIOUS. HARD-WORKING, EASY TO GET ALONG WITH, INTELLIGENT, UNDERSTANDING, SENSITIVE, I COULD GO ON AND ON ABOUT HIM. WE DO NOT HAVE THE SCOPE OF FINANCIAL PROBLEMS THAT I HAD PREVIOUSLY, LEAVING ME LESS STRESS TO DEAL WITH. WE DON'T ARGUE, WE TALK. WE GIVE MUTUALLY AND SHARE EVERYTHING EQUALLY.

THE LACK OF PRESSURE AND WORRY HAS KEPT ME PILL FREE. IT HAS BEEN FOUR YEARS SINCE I TOOK MY LAST BIT OF PILL TO SLEEP AND I SLEEP NOW BETTER THAN EVER BEFORE. I WENT BACK TO SCHOOL

The Courage to Face my Inner Self

AND JUST ACHIEVED MY ASSOCIATE'S DEGREE AND PLAN TO GO ON TO GET MY BACHELORS. I STILL STRUGGLE WITH MOOD SWINGS, BOTH MANIA AND DEPRESSION, BUT HAVE LEARNED SKILLS WITHIN MYSELF TO DEAL WITH THEM AS THEY COME. I TAKE ONE DAY AT A TIME, ONE PROBLEM AT A TIME, AND I DEAL. I DO NOT LOOK AHEAD TOO FAR BECAUSE THAT JUST PUTS PRESSURE ON ME AND I TEND TO PANIC. I HAVE A SCHEDULE THAT I MAKE FOR MYSELF THAT LEAVES LITTLE ROOM FOR SURPRISE. THIS SCHEDULE HELPS ME TO GET WHAT I NEED DONE AND ALLOWS ME TO PLAN WITHOUT FREAKING MYSELF OUT. I

The Courage to Face my Inner Self

mow the lawn on Sundays, wash clothes on Mondays, start dinner at 5:30 and eat at 7:00. I have found that the more I have scheduled and the more I stick to a schedule, the less chance there is that I will have major mood swings.

The Courage to Face my Inner Self

The Courage to Face my Inner Self

The Courage to Face my Inner Self

MIRROR, MIRROR,

ON THE WALL,

HEY,

WHERE DID THAT KID GO?

The Courage to Face my Inner Self

Chapter 8

What I see in the mirror

Learning to deal with how I saw myself over the years has proven difficult. Being treated differently

The Courage to Face my Inner Self

BY OTHERS IS NOT SOMETHING THAT IS EASILY EXPLAINABLE OR EASY TO IGNORE. I CATCH MYSELF QUITE OFTEN NOT GETTING A JOKE, LAUGHING AT THE WRONG TIME OR BEING TOO OUTSPOKEN IN FRONT OF OTHERS. I MAKE OTHER PEOPLE FEEL UNCOMFORTABLE; EVEN THOUGH THAT IS THE LAST THING I WANT TO DO. I FIND MYSELF GRAVITATING TOWARDS PEOPLE THAT ARE DYSFUNCTIONAL BECAUSE THEY ARE THE ONES THAT DON'T SEEM TO MIND MY ODDITIES. LEARNING TO DEAL WITH THIS HAS BEEN DIFFICULT. MY CONCLUSION TO THIS PROBLEM, WHETHER CORRECT OR NOT, IS THAT MY

The Courage to Face my Inner Self

INTELLIGENCE LEVEL IS HIGHER AND THAT PEOPLE JUST DON'T UNDERSTAND ME. I TRY NOT TO PORTRAY THIS TO OTHERS. IF I DID, I MOST LIKELY WOULD HAVE NO FRIENDS AT ALL. WHEN SOMEONE TREATS ME WRONG, INSTEAD OF GETTING MEAN WITH THEM, I JUST THINK TO MYSELF "BOY, IF THEY ONLY KNEW HOW MUCH LESS INTELLIGENT THEY ARE", I MENTALLY LAUGH AND CARRY ON WITH MY LIFE. IT WORKS FOR ME.

The Courage to Face my Inner Self

HEALING BEGINS

WITH ONE'S OWN

PERSONAL HONESTY.

The Courage to Face my Inner Self

Chapter 9

What I left out

I left out quite a bit of my story, most of it fairly monotonous. Things such as I became sexually active early in my life, which led to many short

The Courage to Face my Inner Self

term relationships. I have had many more jobs than the ones mentioned; most of them I left because I would get too mad or upset over dumb stuff. I have two major medical conditions that can be attributed to the various medications I took along my journey, diabetes and leukocytosis. When I get to the point where I need help it either metamorphosis by my mood and actions, like running grocery carts into old people or by causing diarrhea. I frequently use meditation to take myself to a peaceful place to calm my moods.

The Courage to Face my Inner Self

I diet during depression and eat anything during my manic phases. This tends to make me want to be in my manic phase and I think it really helps me shake off the depression. It also keeps me from getting mean during my manic phase. Finally, I have come to the realization that nobody is perfect, we all have our oddities and problems, mine are just different than theirs.

Life is too short to live with this disorder and abuse. The sooner you get out the faster you can stabilize yourself. Medicine is only a tool,

The Courage to Face my Inner Self

THERE IS HOPE. I HAVE TRIED SELF-MEDICATING WITH ALCOHOL, IT DOESN'T WORK, IT ONLY HIDES THE PROBLEM. TRUST YOUR DOCTORS UNTIL YOU REACH THE POINT THAT YOU KNOW 100 PERCENT YOU CAN TRUST IN YOURSELF.

THE BIGGEST THING I LEFT OUT AND THE THING THAT MEANS THE MOST TO ME IS MY CHILDREN. THEY SUFFERED EVERY STEP OF THE WAY ALONG WITH ME. THEY SAW ME UGLY AND THEY SAW ME SAD. THEY SAW THE DAYS THAT I COULDN'T BRING MYSELF TO SHOWER OR DRESS. THEY WITNESSED THE DAYS I WOULD FLY OFF THE HANDLE AT EVERY LITTLE INFRACTION. THEY PUT UP

The Courage to Face my Inner Self

with my dysfunctional relationships and were abused right alongside of me. They were too little to know why all this happened and when they were old enough they didn't care anymore. Recently I have had to face the music over this and I will tell you, it hurts. I thought I was a great parent; I kept a roof over their heads, cooked dinner for them every night, and loved them unconditionally. I can say that we have been talking about these issues and the healing has finally started now that I am in a place where I can see clearly. I love my children with

The Courage to Face my Inner Self

ALL MY HEART AND PRAY FOR TOTAL

FORGIVENESS IN TIME.

The Courage to Face my Inner Self

The Courage to Face my Inner Self

The Courage to Face my Inner Self

Most fears

Lie within our own hearts

And minds.

The Courage to Face my Inner Self

The Conclusion

It is with the deepest wishes that something in my story will help your suffering and lead to a better life. Bi-polar disorder is not something

The Courage to Face my Inner Self

that is fun or fair. I would not wish this on my worst enemy. It is easy to find wrong in others, but not so easy to look within and make changes yourself. One last thing, it is important to find and utilize a good support system, but prepare yourself in the event that you lose them. Many of our loved ones and friends get frustrated and gravitate away from us from lack of understanding. We can't really blame them, but it hurts all the same. Create a routine, even if you start with the small stuff. Finally, live life to the best of your

ABILITY, NOT UP TO OTHERS STANDARDS.

GOD BLESS!

The end

The Courage to Face my Inner Self

Thank you for reading my book. Please feel free to e-mail with any feedback, questions or comments. I look forward to hearing from you!

Regards, Angela

innerselfbipolar@yahoo.com

The Courage to Face my Inner Self

Printed in Great Britain
by Amazon.co.uk, Ltd.,
Marston Gate.